CONTENTS

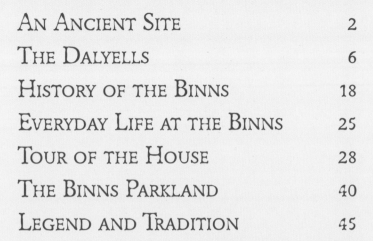

THE HOUSE OF THE BINNS is the only National Trust for Scotland property that is still home to the family whose ancestors first built it. When Eleanor Dalyell gave the Binns to the Trust in 1944, the deed of gift retained the right of the family to live here, under the NTS Country House Scheme. The house and estate are open to the public and the Dalyells, in a partnership arrangement with the Trust, contribute towards its upkeep and maintenance.

The history of the Binns is that of a typical Scottish laird's working estate, rather than a grand stately residence: this, combined with a 'lived in' atmosphere generated by an unbroken continuity of occupation, gives it a unique appeal to visitors today.

AN ANCIENT SITE

The House of the Binns stands high on the western slope of Binns Hill, overlooking the River Forth, with spectacular views in all directions at Scotland's narrowest point. It is easy to understand why this site was chosen from earliest times for habitation, look-out and defence.

The words 'binns', 'bynnis' or 'beinn' are variants on the more familiar 'ben', all old Scots words meaning 'hill'. Reputedly there was an ancient Pictish hill fort behind the house, built on the foundations of a Pictish settlement. Excavations at Cairnpapple Hill, to the south, have revealed a Bronze Age burial and ritual site which is considered one of the most important in mainland Scotland.

An early Christian monastic settlement at nearby Abercorn ('Abercurnig'), beside the River Forth, is mentioned in the Venerable Bede's *Ecclesiastical History of the English Nation*, completed in AD731. It was one of the earliest Christian foundations in Scotland. The twelfth-century church there is still standing, and is the traditional burial place of the Dalyell family, owners of the Binns since the early seventeenth century. In 1618, Thomas Dalyell gained permission from his kinsman the Bishop of Dunkeld, against the wishes of the incumbent minister, to build the Dalyell aisle on to the existing church, so that he and his family could worship there.

The earliest record of the property in the Dalyell family archive dates back to *c*1320, three centuries before the Dalyell name first appears in the area. It is a rent agreement between John Grahame, Lord of Abicorne, and his son Henry, inscribed on vellum in an even Latin script. The rent is defined as '… a pair of gilt spurs, yearly if asked'. Medieval historian Professor Geoffrey Barrow deciphered the text, 'reading it to us, as if from *The Times*,' remember Tam and Kathleen Dalyell. Written evidence exists in the Binns papers of a house prior to 1478, but it is not until the end of the sixteenth century that we have a continuous historical record. In 1599, James, Lord Lindsay 'of Byris, Baron of Abercorn' sold to Sir William Livingstone of Kilsyth, together with other properties, 'the lands of Bynnis and Croceflattis with the manor place thereof'. In 1612 Sir William in turn sold them to Thomas Dalyell, a younger son of the ancient family of Dalzell of Dalzell, later Earls of Carnwath.

The rent agreement of c1320

A Ship That Would Never Sink

Engraving of Blackness Castle from The Beauties of Scotland, *published in 1805*

About one mile to the north of the House of the Binns, on the shores of the River Forth, and clearly seen from Binns Hill, stands Blackness Castle. This formidable bastion guarding Blackness, the old port for Linlithgow, was built in the fifteenth century by the Crichton family.

Its unusual shape, jutting out into the river, is often compared to that of a ship. It is said that James V of Scotland, father of Mary, Queen of Scots, had a Lord High Admiral, Archibald Douglas, who suffered from sea-sickness and was threatened with the removal of his command. Determined to retain his job, since it enabled him to sell lucrative naval posts, he promised in return to build for the King a 'ship that would never sink'. This 'ship' turned out to be Blackness Castle.

In 1453 Blackness became a royal castle, and was used as a fortress and a state prison – the gloomy bottleneck dungeon still exists today. Extensive works in the sixteenth century made it one of the most formidable artillery fortifications in Scotland. During the 'Rough Wooing', when Henry VIII was planning to invade Scotland to capture the young Mary, Queen of Scots as a bride for his son, Sir Ralph Sadler wrote to him in July 1543: 'Governor Arran will ... remove the Queen to Blackness, which is impregnable.'

During the Civil Wars of the seventeenth century the castle was used as a prison for recalcitrant ecclesiastics and during the Napoleonic Wars for French prisoners-of-war. In the nineteenth century it served as a munitions store and barracks. After World War I it became an Ancient Monument conserved by the Office of Works and is now in the care of Historic Scotland. Young children, especially, enjoy running round its battlements and watching the waves splash against the walls of the 'ship'.

The 1612 document of sale between Sir William Livingstone and Thomas Dalyell

The unique interest of the Binns lies in the family that has lived here for nearly 400 years. The house and contents richly reflect their history and, through them, the history of Scotland.

The Dalziels originated in Lanarkshire, where there is to this day a place called Dalziel – the White Dale – near Motherwell. The first to bear the name seems to have been Hugo de Dalzell, Sheriff of Lanark in the late thirteenth century. From him the line descends through Sir William de Dalzell, who lost an eye at the Battle of Otterburn in 1388, and Sir Robert Dalzell, the head of the family, who became Earl of Carnwath in 1628.

'I DARE'

A more romantic version of the origin of the name Dalyell also explains the insignia on the family coat-of-arms. According to this version, a group of Scots invaded England in the early Middle Ages to rescue one of their countrymen who had been imprisoned in Alnwick Castle, just south of the border, in Northumbria. They found his naked corpse strung up on the castle ramparts.

The King of Scots, furious at this insult, asked which of his men would go and retrieve the body of his loyal subject. One of them shouted in response 'I dare!', brandishing a sword in the air. In the ancient Brythonic Celtic tongue his cry sounded like 'Dalyell' – so he and his descendants were known ever after as Dalyell. Their coat-of-arms bore a naked man, an upraised hand with a sword and the motto 'I Dare' – to which a later Dalyell added 'For Right and Reason'.

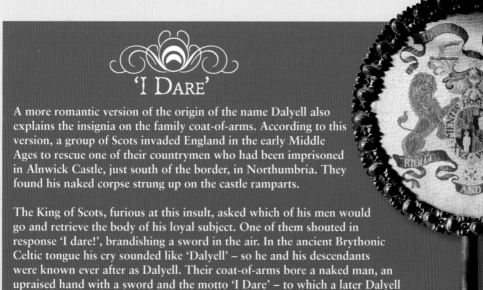

THE DALYELLS

Younger branch of the Dalziels of Lanarkshire (Earls of Carnwath)

THOMAS DALYELL m 1601 JANET BRUCE
(1571-1642)   (1573-1634)

WILLIAM DRUMMOND m 1626 MAGDALENE
of Riccarton

Sir THOMAS DALYELL m 1. KATHERINE DRUMMOND
1st Bart (c1640-1699)   2. AGNES MURRAY

Col THOMAS of
Tichneven in Ireland

Sir THOMAS DALYELL osp
2nd Bart (1675-1719)

WILLIAM
osp (1675-1679)

Sir JAMES MENTEITH DALYELL m Dame HELEN CAMPBELL
3rd Bart (1691-1747)   (-1774)

Sir ROBERT DALYELL m 1773 ELIZABETH GRAHAM
4th Bart (1726-1791)   of Gartmore (-1825)

Captain JAMES (1730-1763)
Died at Fort Detroit

Sir JAMES DALYELL
5th Bart (1774-1841) osp

Sir JOHN GRAHAM DALYELL
6th Bart (1775-1851) osp

General ROBERT
(1776-1848) osp

Sir ROBERT DALYELL
8th Bart (1821-1886) osp

OSBOURNE (1834-1862) osp

MARIA CHRISTINA m 1855 Sir JOHN
(1826-1867)   DU PLATT osp

Sir JAMES BRUCE WILKIE DALYELL m MARY ASKEW-ROBERTSON
9th Bart (1867-1935)   (1870-1947)

ELEANOR DALYELL m 1928 GORDON LOCH
(1895-1972)   (1887-1953)

TAM DALYELL m 1963 KATHLEEN WHEATLEY
10th Bart (1932-)   (1937-)

GORDON DALYELL m 1990 PAMELA LESLIE
(1965-)   (1966-)

MOIRA DALYELL m 1997 IAN SHEARER
(1968-)   (1966-)

MATTHEW THOMAS (2001-)

JAMES NINIAN (2006-)

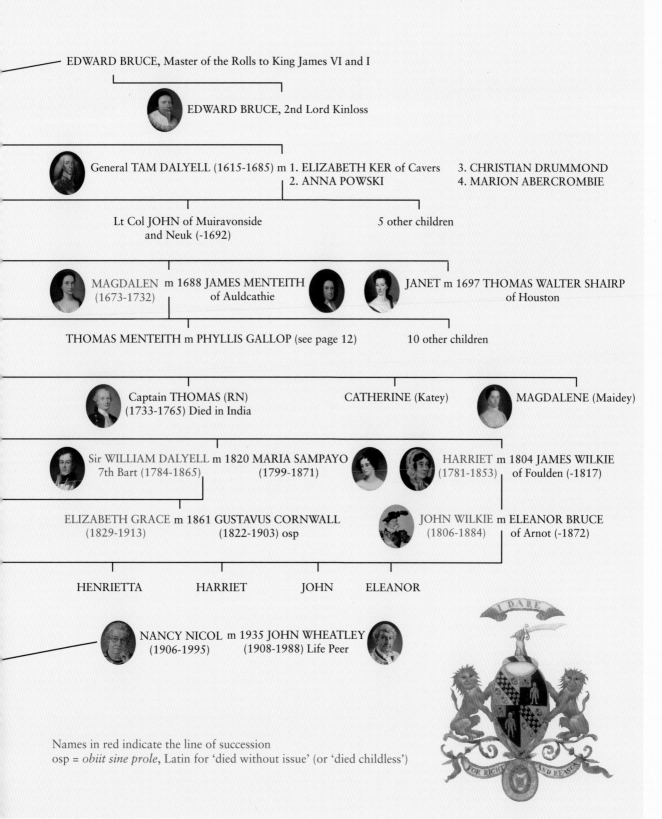

EDWARD BRUCE, Master of the Rolls to King James VI and I

EDWARD BRUCE, 2nd Lord Kinloss

General TAM DALYELL (1615-1685) m 1. ELIZABETH KER of Cavers   3. CHRISTIAN DRUMMOND
                                    2. ANNA POWSKI   4. MARION ABERCROMBIE

Lt Col JOHN of Muiravonside   5 other children
and Neuk (-1692)

MAGDALEN m 1688 JAMES MENTEITH   JANET m 1697 THOMAS WALTER SHAIRP
(1673-1732)   of Auldcathie   of Houston

THOMAS MENTEITH m PHYLLIS GALLOP (see page 12)   10 other children

Captain THOMAS (RN)   CATHERINE (Katey)   MAGDALENE (Maidey)
(1733-1765) Died in India

Sir WILLIAM DALYELL m 1820 MARIA SAMPAYO   HARRIET m 1804 JAMES WILKIE
7th Bart (1784-1865)   (1799-1871)   (1781-1853)   of Foulden (-1817)

ELIZABETH GRACE m 1861 GUSTAVUS CORNWALL   JOHN WILKIE m ELEANOR BRUCE
(1829-1913)   (1822-1903) osp   (1806-1884)   of Arnot (-1872)

HENRIETTA   HARRIET   JOHN   ELEANOR

NANCY NICOL m 1935 JOHN WHEATLEY
(1906-1995)   (1908-1988) Life Peer

Names in red indicate the line of succession
osp = *obiit sine prole*, Latin for 'died without issue' (or 'died childless')

Thomas Dalyell (1571–1642)

Builder of the Binns

Thomas Dalyell, the first of the Binns, was the grandson of a junior branch of the Lanarkshire family that had come to Edinburgh in the sixteenth century. Thomas was a merchant venturer, trading in the northern seas in many commodities – one of which was butter from Orkney, where he had a younger brother, James, collecting the 'butter dett' and shipping it to Leith. There it was sold, at the lower end of the market, for greasing the axle wheels of carts and canons that included the famous Mons Meg, Scotland's biggest gun, still on view at Edinburgh Castle.

Above: Thomas's portrait by George Jamesone, the Aberdeen portrait painter, hangs at the Binns in his 'little studie', now the Business Room. He has a steadfast and canny look, and is dressed simply as if interrupted in doing his accounts

Thomas prospered, becoming a burgess of the city, with a house in Edinburgh's High Street. On 1 August 1601, at Culross Abbey, he married Janet, daughter of Edward Bruce, 1st Baron Kinloss and Senator of the College of Justice, and one of King James VI's most trusted advisors. Both wanted to ensure James's succession to the English throne, which at that time was not certain. The 'front runner' was not James, the Scottish king, son of Mary, Queen of Scots who had been beheaded by Elizabeth, but the Earl of Huntingdon, whose claim was arguably more valid. It is likely that Thomas Dalyell, sailing the seas, carried coded messages between James's supporters.

When James did succeed to the English throne in 1603, he took many Scots with him to London. He created Edward Bruce Master of the Rolls and Bruce, in turn, recruited his young son-in-law Thomas Dalyell as a Deputy Master of the Rolls. These two 'hungrie scottis', like many others at the time, made a great deal of money out of the fact that a King of Scotland had become also a King of England. Thomas was, in effect, a high-powered civil servant, with an important position and great powers of patronage, living in a house with a garden in Fetter Lane. After nine years Thomas was a wealthy man and, on the death of his father-in-law, decided to return to Scotland in 1612. He used his fortune to set himself up as a laird, buying the Binns in the same year.

General Tam Dalyell (1615–85)

'Bloody Tam' or man of culture?

Thomas's son, General Tam Dalyell, dominates the history of the family and of the Binns itself. It was he who introduced thumbikins or thumbscrews into Scotland as instruments of torture, and who was known by the Covenanters as 'Bloody Tam – the Muscovy Brute', allegedly roasting enemies in his bakehouse oven. But he was also called an 'affectionate friend' by Charles II and a 'devoted servant and experienced military specialist' by the Tsar of Russia. His career and character reveal a truly remarkable man of strong principle.

Born at the Binns in 1615, General Tam travelled extensively on the Continent between 1634 and 1637. On his return in 1638 he and his father both signed the National Covenant in Greyfriars Churchyard in Edinburgh. This was a widespread national protest against the forced introduction to Scottish churches of the new Scottish Prayer Book and the imposition of bishops as a form of church government.

But the Dalyells refused, like the Marquis of Montrose, to depart so far from their loyalty to the Crown as to rebel against their King. In the Civil War that followed Tam Dalyell fought on the Royalist side and when Charles I was executed on 30 January 1649, he was so incensed that he took an oath never to cut his hair or his beard until the Stuarts were restored to the throne.

Tam Dalyell was taken prisoner by Cromwell's troops at the Battle of Worcester in 1651, sent to Dudley Castle, and from there to the Tower of London. He is one of the very few to have escaped from that forbidding fortress. The Keeper of the Tower commented acidly in 1969 that his Record Book showed 'Dalyell was not one of our maximum security prisoners' – a Committee of Enquiry, set up in 1652 to discover how he had escaped, has yet to report!

In 1654, when Charles II was holding court in exile at Cologne, General Tam Dalyell received Letters of Recommendation from the King to take service either with John Casimir, King of Poland, or the Tsar of Russia, Alexis Michailovitch. On 21 July 1656, he handed his Letter to the Tsar, who appointed him Commissioner-General in command of the Butyrsky Regiment in Moscow. He fought against the Tartars, Turks and Poles, helped to reform the Tsar's army along the European model, was made a noble of Russia and took a Russian wife, Anna Powski.

Top of page: portrait of General Tam by Schuneman (probably painted c1666). Above: Tsar Alexis Michailovitch. Below: General Tam's spurs

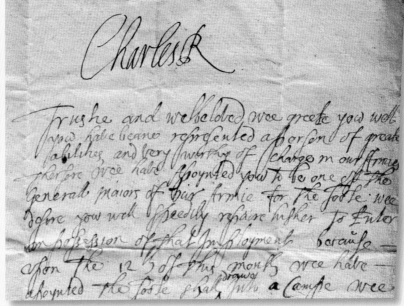

Top of page: portrait of Charles II in the Dining Room and, right, a letter he wrote to General Tam. Above: a recruiting poster of the 1930s for the Royal Scots Greys, the regiment founded by General Tam. Below: General Tam's boots of Russian leather

Part of the General's payment was the award of land, 200 peasant households around Polotsk and the governorship of the great Kremlin at Smolensk. These details were discovered in 1956 by the present Tam Dalyell in the Lenin Library in Moscow, during a National Union of Students visit to Russia. Smolensk was the gateway to Moscow, command of which would not have been given by the Tsar to anyone other than a highly effective general.

After his Restoration in 1660, Charles II needed loyal commanders and in July 1664 he wrote to the Tsar, asking that Dalyell be allowed to return. On 6 January 1665 permission was granted with letters from the Tsar expressing his warm appreciation of General Tam's service.

From 1666, as Commander-in-Chief of the King's forces in Scotland, General Tam confronted the Covenanters – opponents of the King and his religious policy – who had marched on Edinburgh. He defeated them at Rullion Green in the Pentlands, in 1666, but gave orders that some 30 women and children following their army should be spared. This was overruled by Lord Lauderdale, Scottish Secretary of State, whose harsh rule had done much to inflame the rebellion. So incensed was Dalyell that he resigned his commission and retired from public office. He withdrew to the Binns to devote himself to experiments in gardening and arboriculture that place him a century in advance of his time.

After ten years of retirement, General Tam was called back to public office by his King to help restore order to a troubled land. From then until his death in 1685 he was active against the rebellious Covenanters during a period of harsh repression known as 'The Killing Times'.

In order to pursue this campaign, he raised troops of dragoons in 1678 and 1681, which became the famous Scottish Regiment, the Royal Scots Greys (now the Royal Scots Dragoon Guards).

Charles II had intended to grant a baronetcy to General Tam for his services. However, both died before this could be finalised, so the baronetcy of Nova Scotia was conferred on the general's son by James II. By a special deposition it passes through 'heirs male and tailzie' – that is, through the female line in default of male heirs.

On 23 August 1685, as reported in the Inventory made at the Binns following his death, 'the Good Old General died of ane apoplexie [a stroke]' in his house in Edinburgh, and a week later was given a full military funeral, conducted as ordered by the Privy Council. The detailed instructions for the procession, and a list of the funeral costs, can be seen in the house.

The Inventory of 1685, listing all the contents of the Binns, was published in 1924 in the *Proceedings of the Society of the Antiquaries of Scotland*, and the introduction by Sir James Dalyell and James Beveridge pointed out how it revealed a character far removed from the traditional perception of the general.

'The inventory presents a picture widely different from the figure in popular tradition of a rough, brutal soldier of fortune, coarse in manners, slovenly in dress … who roasted alive his miserable prisoners and played cards with the devil. We find a gentleman of taste and comparative refinement, far superior to what prevailed among contemporaries of his rank and station. With a mind enriched by foreign travel, he surrounded himself, both at The Binns and in his town house in the Canongate in Edinburgh, with a luxury that was uncommon in Scotland in his day.'

A coloured lithograph of troops of the Greys by J W Giles, mid-nineteenth century Below: Pilkington Jackson's plaster figures of the Scots Greys stand in the Laigh Hall

THE PHANTOM ARMY

According to Dalyell family tradition the name of the Royal Scots Greys derives from the colour not of their horses, but of their uniform, devised by their first Colonel-in-Chief, General Tam Dalyell.

General Tam's Russian experience had taught him the importance of camouflage. He had seen how effectively the Poles had used white uniforms against the snow and thought grey would be equally effective against the background of the Scottish countryside and weather. He sent to Flanders for 2,536 ells of grey cloth for uniforms for his new regiment. His dragoons were known as the 'Phantom Army' as they flitted through the Border landscape in their grey uniforms. Three centuries later, in 1974, they were amalgamated with the 3rd Carabiniers to form the Royal Scots Dragoon Guards, and have recently seen service in Bosnia, Kosovo and Iraq.

MAGDALEN DALYELL (1673–1732)

The American Connection

One of the advantages of living in a house open to the public is that visitors often contribute golden nuggets of information. An American visitor surmised there was a link between the Dalyells and the family of the 33rd President of the United States – Harry S Truman.

Above: Magdalen's portrait by William Aikman, which hangs at the Binns, reveals a small, dark, formidable woman, thin of lip, straight of back, determination in every bone – once a beauty and clearly a Dalyell. Still in the house are the last of 'a set of hingings for the haille hoose' that she and her daughters made up from imported Indian cloth, along with her little gold thimble (opposite page)

On a visit to Boston and the Genealogical Society of New England, Kathleen Dalyell learnt the exact nature of the link. General Tam's granddaughter, Magdalen Dalyell, married a neighbour, James Menteith of Auldcathie, in 1688, at the age of 15. She bore him a dozen children – six sons and six daughters. When her brother, Sir Thomas Dalyell the 2nd Baronet, died in 1719, she succeeded as heir of tailzie, though she had to pursue a court case to do so. On the death of her husband, after some years running the Binns estates, she handed over to her son, Sir James Menteith Dalyell, 3rd Baronet, and set off from Glasgow to Virginia with her younger children, dying there at Rappahannock of a fever in 1732.

Her second son, Thomas Menteith, who kept his father's name, married Phyllis Gallop in Rappahannock. Their daughter, another Magdalen, married Anderson Doniphan and produced a daughter, Elizabeth, who married Richard Shipp. The Shipps moved from Virginia to Kentucky, and their daughter, Emma Shipp, married William Truman. Their son, Anderson Shipp Truman, moved further west from Kentucky to Missouri, where his son, John Anderson Truman, fathered Harry S Truman, born in 1884.

THE TRUMAN CONNECTION

THOMAS MENTEITH m PHYLLIS GALLOP
|
MAGDALEN MENTEITH m ANDERSON DONIPHAN
|
ELIZABETH DONIPHAN m RICHARD JONATHAN SHIPP
|
EMMA SHIPP m WILLIAM TRUMAN
|
ANDERSON SHIPP TRUMAN
|
JOHN ANDERSON TRUMAN
|
HARRY S TRUMAN
33rd President of the United States (1945-1953)

Captain James Dalyell (1730–63)

A Violent End

One of Magdalen's Scottish grandsons went to America some 30 years after her death. Captain James Dalyell, the younger brother of Sir Robert Dalyell, 4th Baronet, joined the army to find fame and fortune. In the mid-eighteenth century, during the Seven Years War between Britain and France, James was aide-de-camp to Sir Jeffrey Amherst, the Commander-in-Chief of the British forces in North America, and distinguished himself fighting against the French and their native American allies.

Above: James's portrait at the Binns, by Cosmo Alexander, shows an elegant young man in a red waistcoat. Below: letter from Captain James Dalyell to his brother, Sir Robert, written in the year he was killed

His reputation among his fellow officers as being full of enthusiasm, brave and reckless is borne out by his letters home to his brother. They tell of his plans for setting up a model colony after the wars, describe the special type of swivel gun he had devised to use on boats as they moved up river, and reveal how he was courting a general's daughter – 'but hush to mama about that'.

James was killed in July 1763, at the age of 33, just outside Fort Detroit in a particularly fierce engagement known as Bloody Run. Determined to deliver a devastating blow to the Ottawa Indians under Pontiac, who had pinned down the British in their forts, James insisted on mounting a surprise night-time attack. French spies had warned the enemy and the majority of his 250 men were massacred, including the Captain himself, who had gone to help his injured sergeant. Riddled with bullets and arrows, James was scalped. His heart was removed, roasted and given to Pontiac to eat. The Ottawas believed that the bravery of the young Scotsman would thereby be transmitted to their Chief.

James is buried to the rear of the present First National Bank of Detroit. The mystics in the family swear they have seen him around the house.

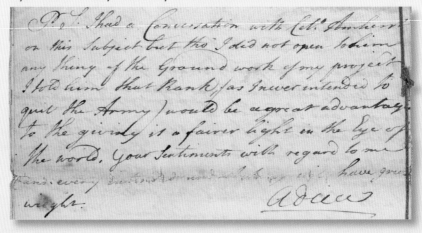

Sir John Graham Dalyell (1775-1851)

Teacher of Darwin

The most scholarly of the Dalyells, Sir John was knighted for his services to literature and science before succeeding his brother as 6th Baronet in 1841. Lamed for life as a child by a fall at the Binns, he could not follow the more energetic family careers of the army, navy or diplomatic service. A member of the Faculty of Advocates, he practised law from home, never taking a fee from a relative, a widow or an orphan.

He studied a wide range of subjects including antiquities, history, music and musical instruments, the devil and superstition, but above all natural history. His publications were extensive and meticulous but it is his *Rare and Remarkable Animals of Scotland*, beautifully illustrated by his sister, Elizabeth, that is his greatest and best-known work.

A fragment of hers among the Binns papers reveals a strange perception of the respective roles of men and women, or else a wicked sense of humour: 'It was a curious fact that you have not put my name as the authority or observer, for nothing looks so bad as a woman's name in any book ... more particularly a book of profound learning, observation or deep study.'

A well-known and respected figure in Edinburgh, Sir John had many friends, including Sir Walter Scott. Sir John taught Darwin when he was at Edinburgh University and may have been among those in the Science Faculty who turned Darwin's interest away from medicine towards the study of natural history.

Sir John gathered many specimens, the most noted of which was a pet sea anemone called 'Grannie', which he collected at North Berwick in 1828. He fed this hermaphrodite creature on mussels, observing and recording its activity, noting that it produced 230 young in the course of one night and then nothing for 16 years! On Sir John's death in 1851, 'Grannie' was passed round his friends to be looked after until 'she' died 36 years later, meriting obituaries in *The Times* and *The Scotsman*.

Sir John was particularly interested in the reproductive powers of the common leech and his studies on flatworms resulted in one of the rhabdocoele family being called *Dalyelliidae* after him.

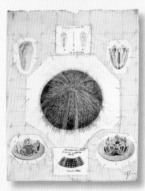

Top of page: portrait of Sir John Graham Dalyell by an unknown artist. Above: two of Elizabeth Dalyell's fine illustrations to her brother's book

Sir William Dalyell (1784–1865)

War Hero

The youngest son of Sir Robert Dalyell the 4th Baronet, William succeeded his two elder brothers as 7th Baronet in 1851. Entering the navy at the age of nine, Midshipman – later Admiral – William Dalyell had a series of remarkable adventures that provided C S Forester with some of the material for his *Hornblower* stories.

Above: William's portrait by Lauri Girard at the Binns shows a dark, handsome man in his admiral's uniform, the scars from the sabre wounds visible on his forehead. Below: Thomas Lawrence's portrait of William's wife Maria and, at foot of page, the sword presented to William by the Patriotic Fund

During the Napoleonic Wars, William distinguished himself in a series of expeditions to capture enemy ships off the French coast. On 4 January, 1805, with three small boats and 27 volunteers, he endeavoured to bring out a notorious privateer, the *Vimereux*, from her anchorage in the bay of St Valery-en-Caux, not knowing it was a French trap. Only six of the British expedition escaped unhurt: the rest were either killed or wounded. William Dalyell was conveyed to a dungeon with nine sabre wounds on his head and severe lacerations all over his body. He was saved from the death cart by the intervention of a French doctor, who nursed him back to health. After six months, he landed in a prisoner-of-war camp at Verdun. It was not until the end of the war in 1814 that he was released to return home to his family. Believing him dead, they had gone into deep mourning, until he had managed to scrawl a few lines to them from prison.

The Patriotic Fund presented William with a 50-guinea sword and 100 guineas for his valour in the engagement of 1805. He was never to see service again but was awarded a pension of 5 shillings a day, later increased to 150 guineas a year. He was promoted to the rank of Commander and eventually became one of the Governors of Greenwich Hospital in 1840. In September 1820 he married Maria Sampayo and by her had four children.

Sir James Bruce Wilkie Dalyell (1867–1935)
& Eleanor Dalyell (1895–1972)

The 9th Baronet, Sir James Bruce Wilkie Dalyell, served in the South African War (1899-1901) and was mentioned in dispatches. In 1913 he succeeded his cousin Elizabeth Grace Cornwall Dalyell, daughter of Sir William Dalyell, 7th Baronet, and, selling his estates of Foulden in Berwickshire, moved to the Binns.

When World War I broke out in 1914 he rejoined his unit, the King's Own Scottish Borderers, and served with distinction in Egypt and Gallipoli. Never in good health thereafter, he worked on the family papers at the Binns along with James Beveridge, the scholarly Rector of Linlithgow Academy. Their work resulted in the publication of the Binns Papers by the Scottish Record Society.

On his death in 1935 his daughter and heir of tailzie, Eleanor, succeeded to the land and titles of the Binns. On 9 November 1944, Eleanor Dalyell gifted the House of the Binns, its contents and the parklands, together with an endowment for their upkeep, to the National Trust for Scotland under the Trust's Country House Scheme.

Above: portraits of Sir James, by Edward Drummond Young, and of Eleanor, by Stanley Cursiter. Below: the present Tam Dalyell as a small boy at the Binns in 1937, with the Sheikh of Bahrain

Eleanor Dalyell died on 5 February 1972. The long and happy association between the family and the Trust continues with Tam Dalyell, the son of Eleanor and Gordon Loch (who took the name and designation of Dalyell). Tam, the 10th Baronet, who does not use the title, was educated first at the Edinburgh Academy, then at Eton and Cambridge before qualifying in Edinburgh as a teacher. After four years at Bo'ness Academy, he became deputy director of the ship school *Dunera*. For 37 years he was a columnist for the *New Scientist*. In June 1962 he was elected Member of Parliament for his home constituency of West Lothian, now Linlithgow – the constituency that his ancestor General Tam Dalyell had represented 300 years previously. After 43 years as MP, the last five as Father of the House of Commons, he retired from Parliament in 2005.

HISTORY OF THE BINNS

Despite later additions, the present House of the Binns is still very much the house Thomas Dalyell built in the early seventeenth century. An estate only four miles from the king's palace at Linlithgow and due south of Blackness, then one of Scotland's busiest harbours, was clearly an asset. But what Thomas found at the Binns to build upon and adapt to his needs is difficult to determine. It looks as if there were indeed a group of very old buildings that form the two wings to the south, along with early medieval buildings. Architectural features within the present house indicate a tower in the north-west corner, predating Thomas's but incorporated by him into his new house.

Whatever its history, by the time Thomas bought 'the land of bynnis and the manor place thereof' for 38,000 merks (just over £2,000) the structure was not of importance within the district and Thomas lived at the nearby tower house at Mannerston while his new home was being built. We do not know how long this took – tradition says between 1612 and 1630 when the plaster ceilings were installed. Above a window on the west façade is the date 1621 and in the Laigh Hall, above the fireplace, is the date 1622, which may be when the Dalyells took entry. Thomas's initials, intertwined with those of his wife, Janet Bruce, can be seen inside and outside the house, over doorways and fireplaces and on ceilings.

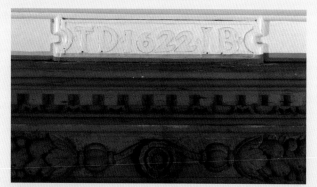

Top: the initials of Thomas Dalyell and Janet Bruce carved above the fireplace in the Laigh Hall. Above: Blackness Castle from the Binns, showing its 'ship' profile distinctly

Above: General Tam Dalyell, 1615-85, by David Paton. Below: William Lawson's paintings of the House of the Binns from the north (top) and south, c1830

The new house was a tall grey three-storeyed building, long and narrow, each room the width of the house, with small mullioned and half-shuttered windows. The steep pitched roof sheltered little dormer windows and, on the north side, at both ends, were twin stair turrets topped by pepper-pot roofs.

The main entrance was then on the south side, where two wings protruded to create a U-shaped building round a cobbled courtyard. To the east, possibly detached from the main building, was a service wing with a vaulted bakehouse, brewhouse, saddle-house and stables with unmarried men's quarters above. To the west were the dairy, larder and cellars with, above, the unmarried women's quarters.

In the later seventeenth century, Thomas Dalyell's son, General Tam Dalyell, devoted himself to tending his estate in a period of temporary retirement from his military exploits, from 1668 to 1678. He certainly had a garden, facing south and west at the bend on the present west drive by which visitors approach the house. His portrait in the Blue Room at the house bears an inscription that quotes from *Camden's Britannica*, the first topographical survey of Great Britain, by William Camden, first published in 1610 and updated in 1695:

'After he had procured himself a lasting name in the wars, here it was that he rested in his old age, and pleased himself with the culture of curious flowers and plants.'

The last of the General's gnarled cherry trees was destroyed in 1998.

In 1745 Sir Robert Dalyell, the 4th Baronet, extended and embellished the house into the form you see today. He added the present Morning Room and Dining Room on the site of the old cobbled court. The level of the court was raised to create an upper and lower terrace with a walk along the old driveway to a newly-created walled garden. The southern side of the house became the rear of the building and the main entrance transferred to the north, giving direct entrance to the present Laigh Hall, formed from the old Laigh Hall and the original Dining Room.

The 300-acre parkland designed by Sir Robert, though some of its features have been lost, is one of very few designed landscapes of this period owned by the National Trust for Scotland. Many trees planted at this time still stand, and were listed comprehensively in 1992: they include beech, chestnut, lime, oak, sycamore and willow. Sir Robert started work on the walled garden, which included an orchard and a fish pond, with a path linking it to the mansion house on the south side.

Sir Robert's son, Sir James, 5th Baronet, continued these 'improvements' between 1810 and 1830. The east and west ranges of the house were enlarged and the pepper-pot turrets gave way to crenellations in the 'Gothick' style then popular, which also inspired the conifer plantings and the tower and gate lodges (now gone) in the parkland. Sir James was a friend of the Romantic novelist Sir Walter Scott, who visited the Binns and doubtless influenced these decisions. It is thought that the renowned architect William Burn, or possibly his father Robert, was consulted. The two contemporary paintings on the stairway in the present house, traditionally held to be blueprints, show the proposed alterations from the north and the south.

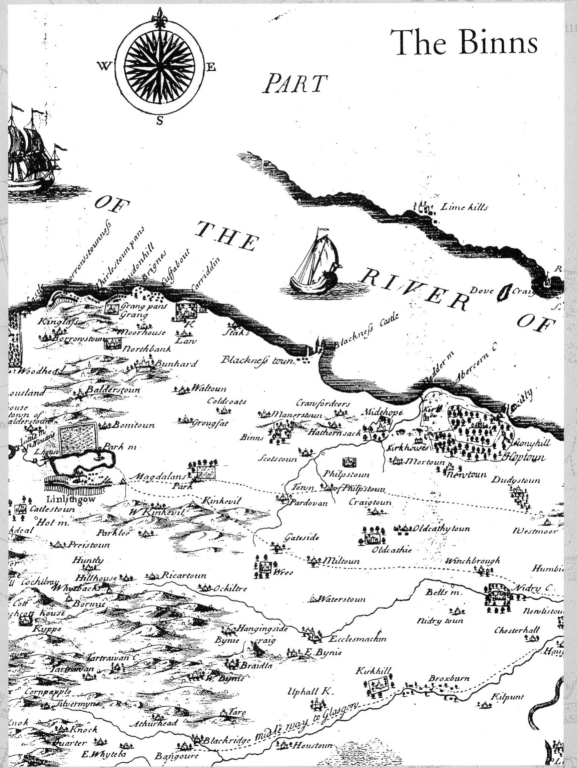

Above: John Adair's Map of West Lothian, 1737, in which the Binns can be seen, south of Blackness Castle

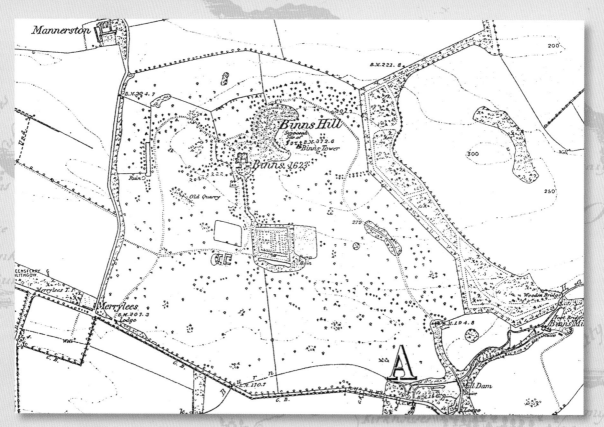

The same Sir James made a notable addition to the landscape – the tower on the hill above the house, which he built in 1826 for £29.10s from the proceeds of an after-dinner wager. Nearly a century later, the 9th Baronet, Sir James Bruce Wilkie Dalyell, added a windmill to the tower to generate electricity.

The two driveways leading to the house, one tarmacked and in use, the other now grassed over but visible and suitable for agricultural vehicles, were built at the instigation of Sir John Graham Dalyell (1775-1851). His aim was partly to provide employment for immigrant workers from Ireland, who came to Scotland in the late 1840s as a consequence of the disastrous potato famine in Donegal, Cork, Kerry and Wexford.

All the additions made in the nineteenth century exhausted the family fortunes. Land had to be sold to pay for them and the lifestyle they engendered – some to the neighbouring Hope family, who had made a fortune as distinguished bankers to the kings of Scotland. The Hopes commissioned Sir William Bruce to design a magnificent mansion, Hopetoun House, in 1699. Thirty years later, it was expanded and embellished by William, John and Robert Adam and set in grounds landscaped in the grand eighteenth-century manner.

Top: the First Edition Ordnance Survey map of 1855 shows the Binns estate in its heyday. Above: postcard of the late 1920s or early 1930s, showing the windmill then on the tower

A considerable part of the Binns estate to the north and west of the house was sold in 1920 under compulsory purchase by the Department of Agriculture to provide smallholdings for soldiers returning from World War I. The nineteenth-century lodges at the entrance of the drives were replaced in 1935 by the existing West Lodge and the gardener's cottage, designed by the young Basil Spence.

Towards the end of World War II, Eleanor Dalyell was approached by the infant National Trust for Scotland, represented by the chairman, Sir Iain Colquhoun of Luss, KT, the honorary secretary, Colonel Sir Edward Stevenson, the treasurer, Arthur Russell of Strathearn & Blair, and the Dalyell family solicitor, (later Sir) Ernest Wedderburn DKS of Shepherd & Wedderburn. They proposed that she should give the Binns to the Trust as their first property under the embryo Country House Scheme, which allowed the owners to continue living in their house. The Binns had been chosen as an 'experiment' because of its proximity to Edinburgh, the good condition of the house, and because there were no complications about family inheritance. As the war ended, in which so much had been lost, Eleanor and her husband Gordon readily agreed to this means of conserving their historic family home.

Top: photograph of the house c1900, by John Nicol. Above: the East Lodge gateway photographed about ten years before its demolition c1960

PRESERVED FOR ALL TIME

April 1946: Eleanor Dalyell hands the deeds of the Binns estate to David, Earl of Wemyss, vice-chairman of the National Trust for Scotland. The Charter of Gift carried the signature of 13-year-old Tam Dalyell (wearing a kilt in the photograph on the right), alongside those of his parents. It stated:

'Considering that I am in sympathy with the purposes and aims of The National Trust for Scotland ... and that I am desirous that the Binns with its history and legend and the memory of the family of Dalyell of the Binns shall be preserved for all time coming for the benefit and enjoyment of the Nation and that I have resolved to grant a Charter ... reserving always ... the sole right to use the territorial designation of the Binns and to fly at the Binns if and when in residence there the armorial Banner of Dalyell of the Binns and to hold the Baron Court in the Laigh Hall of the Binns and to appoint the Baron Baillie and Baron Officer ... and the right to the hidden treasure of the Binns should it be recovered.'

Above: Tam and Kathleen Dalyell at home at the Binns

In 1948, the UK Committee on the Preservation of Historic Houses, set up by Hugh Dalton, Labour Chancellor of the Exchequer, visited the Binns. This hard-nosed, experienced committee was chaired by Sir Ernest Gowers GBE and included James Lees-Milne, scholar and later adviser on Historic Buildings to the English National Trust. They endorsed the arrangement at the Binns, whereby the family and the National Trust for Scotland could work in partnership, sharing the costs and administration of opening the house to the public.

The Binns is the only NTS property where the Country House Scheme continues to operate. Tam and Kathleen Dalyell live with their family in the house, acting, on a voluntary basis, as the NTS representatives. They continue to contribute to the upkeep and maintenance and add to the collections within the house, sometimes by commissioning work. They have also set up the archive room, containing historical documents and photographs relating to the Binns. But above all it is their family home, in which they live and work, welcoming their friends as well as visitors.

EVERYDAY LIFE AT THE BINNS

The house built by the first Thomas Dalyell was designed as the centre of a working estate and to accommodate his family, his extended family and servants – about 30/40 persons in all. The household was a self-sufficient community that provided for most of its own needs, baking bread, brewing ale and making butter. Meat and fish had to be salted to preserve it for consumption during winter, as no fresh meat was then available, except for the pigeons in the laird's dovecot.

Above: an inventory drawn up
when the Dowager Countess of
Traquair leased the house in 1749

The seventeenth-century household would have had a large retinue of busy servants ensuring that the estate ran smoothly. The old documents at the Binns reveal a great deal about their activities. In addition to the ordinary household duties, the women looked after the poultry, the bees, and the cattle in the byre, and worked in the bakery, the brewery and the dairy. The winter evenings found them carding and spinning home-grown wool and flax. The men attended to the riding and work-horses, worked on the home farm and, in General Tam's day, carried out the everyday tasks associated with his hobbies of gardening and planting.

Evidence suggests that the Dalyells of this period entertained on a lavish scale. The Inventory of 1685 lists, along with all the room contents, the 'hurly' beds kept under the main beds and hurled (wheeled) out when needed for guests, who were often forced to stay because of inclement weather. At a time when most lairds possessed only one wineglass, the Binns was unusual in having an ample supply of drinking vessels: 5 dozen cups, either silver or silver-mounted; over 5 dozen glasses; plus pewter vessels, wooden drinking-cans, stoups and quaichs. These were always of matching design, as was the furniture, fabric materials and colours of the High Hall and the bedrooms, indicating provision for many and regular guests.

At the dinner-table there would be no forks (there was only one large fork in the house), but there was a large stock of 24 dozen napkins. The napery, along with clothes not in daily use, were stored mostly in trunks. The sanitary arrangements would be primitive: according to the Binns Inventory of 1685, ladies washed their hands once a day and their faces once a week.

The 1685 Inventory also reveals that the walls were hung with trophies and curios, especially of foreign weapons collected on General Tam's travels abroad. A well-stocked armoury contained 20 swords of different kinds, 12 pikes, 7 pistols and 32 guns. The family and their guests had at their disposal golf clubs and chess boards with their pieces, along with equipment for shooting, hawking, hunting and curling. Surprisingly, no playing cards are listed in the Inventory.

Over the years the number of servants at the Binns dwindled. Their names appear on documents in the archives as witnesses to transactions, but it is difficult to estimate the number at any one given time. This is compounded by the fact that the Dalyells, in the eighteenth and nineteenth centuries, also had homes in Edinburgh, London and Greenwich, as well as travelling abroad.

Mrs Cornwall Dalyell, who died in 1913, employed Charlie Grey as a gardener for over four decades and remembered him in her will. There is also a record of a companion, Madame Bleu. But during World War I the family occupancy was interrupted when the house was leased out to naval personnel from Rosyth. This resulted in a break in any oral tradition that might have been forthcoming from servants and others.

In between the wars the staff was reduced to a general factotum, a gardener, a cook and two girls. A nanny appeared in 1932 to deal with the young Tam Dalyell when his mother departed with her husband to Arabia; then a Swiss Mademoiselle Etter arrived for a couple of years, prior to his going to school at the age of six.

In living memory, the estate factotum was Bert Norton, an Englishman who saw action at Gallipoli in World War I, alongside Sir James Bruce Wilkie Dalyell. A bond was established between the two, and when the war ended Dalyell offered Norton employment, which lasted from 1919 to 1939. Norton was also the chauffeur for a lumbering Teroplane car. He was treated, not as a servant, but as the Company Sergeant-Major that he once had been. The gardener, Joseph Paterson, had fought in Flanders and was treated in a similar military fashion.

The present staff consists of an NTS conservation cleaner, an NTS gardener and seasonal guides, along with the family cleaner, handyman and gardener.

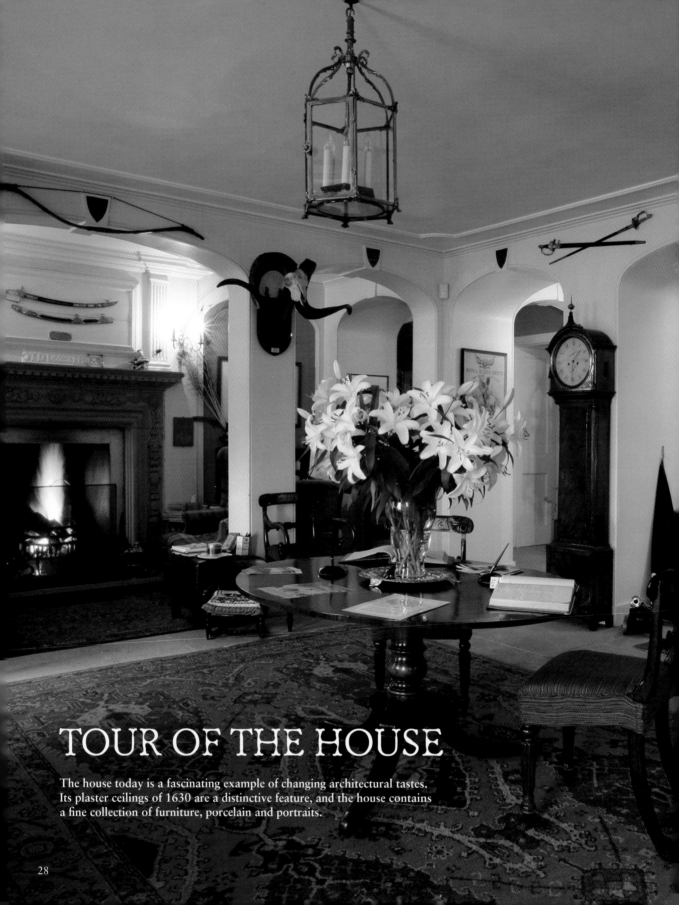

TOUR OF THE HOUSE

The house today is a fascinating example of changing architectural tastes.
Its plaster ceilings of 1630 are a distinctive feature, and the house contains
a fine collection of furniture, porcelain and portraits.

The Laigh (Low) Hall

In Thomas's original house of 1612-30 this was two rooms: the Entrance Hall and the Dining Room. The original seventeenth-century fireplace, decorated with swags of fruit, remains on the east wall. Above the fireplace are the initials TD & IB for Thomas Dalyell and his wife Janet Bruce, the builders of the house, on either side of the date 1622.

According to the Inventory of 1685, the Dining Room, with two windows facing south and two facing north, was furnished with a table and ten chairs of Russian leather for family meals. Serious entertaining was done in the High Hall above.

In the mid-eighteenth century, Sir Robert Dalyell, 4th Baronet, combined the two rooms into a larger Laigh Hall, with its arcade of pillars on three sides, and introduced the present entrance in the north wall. Around the arcades he set painted shields with the coats-of-arms of families that had married into the Dalyells, such as the Bruces and the Menteiths.

Above: Sergeant Ewart of the Scots Greys at the Battle of Waterloo by Christopher Clark (1875-1942)

Above the fireplace hangs the 50-guinea presentation sword awarded by the Patriotic Fund to Sir William Dalyell for his heroism in 1805, during the Napoleonic Wars. Only 80 of them were made, by R Teed of The Strand in London.

The bridal, or 'hope' chest, so called as such chests were often used by young girls to store their trousseaux, could very well have started life bringing the armorial china and tea in a clipper ship from the Far East. The two plaster figures of Scots Greys are by Pilkington Jackson, the well-known Scottish sculptor of, among other works, the statue of Robert the Bruce at Bannockburn. One shows a Grey as he would have been accoutred in the 1680s, the other at the time of the Marlborough Wars in the early eighteenth century.

On the west wall, you can see a fine Jacobean chest, above which is the oil painting by Christopher Clark of Sergeant (later Ensign) Ewart of the Scots Greys capturing the French 45th Regiment Standard at the Battle of Waterloo on 18 June 1815. On the opposite wall there is an engraving by Caton Woodville of the Greys commandeering the horses of the local Gendarmerie on landing in Flanders in 1694.

The Russian samovar and the Turkish coffee pot, along with the Turkish coffee tables by the fireplace, were brought back by Sir Robert Dalyell, 8th Baronet, who spent many years as a diplomat in the Middle East.

Three of the four heads of ibex were shot in the 1920s by Colonel Gordon Loch in Gilgit in the North-West Frontier region of India. Notice the strange twisted horn of the remaining one, which he found and brought back as a curiosity, showing that the animal somehow managed to live a considerable time after the accident that caused the malformation.

The seventeenth-century Carrara marble-topped table is that on which General Tam is said to have played cards with the Devil: you can find out more about this story in the section 'Legend and Tradition' on page 45.

As you go from the Laigh Hall through into the Blue Room, notice on your left, behind a panelled door, the entrance to a secret passage that is traditionally held to burrow a mile underground, surfacing on the riverbank at Blackness. In the seventeenth century, this was an escape route from the house, later used for smuggling. Sir Robert Dalyell had it blocked up for safety reasons in 1881.

THE BLUE ROOM

This was General Tam's own room. It derives its name from the collection of blue-and-white porcelain displayed on the panelled walls, which contains fine examples of Chinese willow pattern porcelain, English Worcester and Dutch delft.

During the redecoration of 1990, early seventeenth-century panelling and two secret cupboards were discovered behind the late seventeenth-century bolection moulding. The older panelling is decorated with paintings of an upraised hand holding a sword – the insignia of the Dalyell family. We assume that this was commissioned by Thomas Dalyell, the builder of the house, but covered up in General Tam's time by the panelling you see now.

The present colour scheme, created during the 1990 redecoration, corresponds to the earliest colour found beneath over 20 layers of paint.

Above the original seventeenth-century stone fireplace is the bearded portrait of General Tam Dalyell by David Paton, illustrating how he kept his oath never to cut his hair or shave after the execution of Charles I.

The Business Room/Little Studie

Like the Blue Room, this 'little studie' has retained its fine late seventeenth-century bolection moulded panelling. The door in the north wall provided easy access to the laird for tenants and workers.

Above the fireplace is a portrait by George Jamesone, the Aberdeen painter, of Thomas Dalyell, the butter merchant who founded the family fortunes and built the house. Note also the etching of Tsar Alexis Michailovitch, with whom General Tam took service.

Perhaps the most interesting feature of this room is the shelving, concealed behind the panelling – a rare seventeenth-century survival. Here, General Tam Dalyell kept his library. This 'bibliothick', as it was called in the 1685 Inventory, contained books on Latin, Greek, philosophy, military strategy and horticulture, and all the books were listed in a catalogue. It had a ladder to reach the topmost shelves.

The Accounts/Telephone Room

This room was created during the renovations of the eighteenth and early nineteenth centuries, filling in an archway that previously gave access from the stables to the original entrance on the south side.

The leather-bound luggage accompanied Harriet Dalyell on her honeymoon, after her marriage to James Wilkie of Foulden in 1804. The paintings are of Sir James Dalyell, 5th Baronet and Sir John Graham Dalyell, 6th Baronet.

THE SMOKING ROOM

This barrel-vaulted room was originally part of the bakehouse/brewhouse arrangement within the east wing, but in the nineteenth century it became a Smoking Room, where the gentlemen gathered after dinner to smoke their cigars and talk, well away from the ladies in the Drawing Room.

The sporting painting by Sartorius is of Eclipse, the most famous Derby winner of all time, who was never beaten in a race. He sired many other champion horses and, according to the Royal Veterinary College, around 80 per cent of modern thoroughbred racehorses have Eclipse in their pedigree, including the celebrated Grand National winner Red Rum.

The cartoons of nineteenth-century celebrities are by Leslie Ward, known as 'Spy', from *Vanity Fair*. You can spot caricatures of Baden-Powell, Lord Rosebery and Lord Kitchener, among others.

Above left: a cartoon by Griffin in The Guardian *newspaper. It depicted Tam Dalyell's dogged pursuit of Prime Minister Margaret Thatcher in the House of Commons, to uncover the facts about the sinking of the Argentine ship, the* Belgrano, *during the Falklands War in 1982. Below: Francis Sartorius' portrait of the famous late eighteenth-century Derby winner, 'Eclipse'*

THE BAKEHOUSE

This is one of the oldest rooms in the house, with its thick old walls and barrel-vaulted ceiling. The large bread oven, 8 ft in diameter, would have burned wood. Once it was hot enough for baking, the embers would be raked out and dough put in with the wooden 'peel', or shovel, that you can see alongside the oven. The small oven to the left was heated from the larger oven, and was used for keeping salt dry, warming plates or raising dough.

On the dresser is a fine collection of seventeenth-century pewter. The items around the Bakehouse were found in attics and outhouses where they had been stored once no longer in use. They include a 'girnel', or chest, for storing flour and meal, a roasting jack for turning the spit, Victorian range kettles, a knife cleaner, a bed warmer, an ice-cream maker and jelly pans.

THE MORNING ROOM

This and the adjoining Dining Room were built on in 1745 by Sir Robert Dalyell, the 4th Baronet.

The breakfront bookcase contains the armorial china, with the family coat-of-arms and the motto 'I Dare for Right and Reason'. About 60 per cent is Chinese export, imported from Canton to Lowestoft, and the remainder English Derby.

Top: the Bakehouse and (above) the bread oven. Below: the Morning Room

THE DINING ROOM

This room has some fine pieces of Scottish furniture, dating from the late eighteenth and early nineteenth centuries. The curtains are kelims (woven rugs) brought back from the East by Sir Robert Dalyell, the 8th baronet, who was British Consul in Erzeroum, in the Armenian region of the Ottoman Empire, in the mid-nineteenth century. These are so distinctive that a group of Turkish parliamentarians visiting the house in recent years was able to identify the family that made them, and the village where they lived.

Around the walls are family portraits, the most striking of which is that of General Tam Dalyell as Commander-in-Chief of the King's Forces in Scotland. It was probably painted by the German artist Schuneman (who painted a similar portrait in the Scottish National Portrait Gallery). Mementoes of General Tam can be seen around this room: above the fireplace are his boots of Russian leather and his fifteenth-century double-handed sword – a present from the Tsar of Russia. His stool of Russian leather and his little campaign chest covered with sealskins are also here.

In the glass case are displayed the huge comb he used on his long hair, his spurs, his dirk, his silver camp spoon engraved with his name, and a gilt Nuremberg cup said to have also been a gift from the Tsar. His Bible of 1611 is one of the earliest in the Scots vernacular.

On either side of General Tam hang portraits of two of his sons – on the left, a painting by Sir John Medina of Thomas, the 1st Baronet and the ancestor of the present family, and on the right, John, a younger son, the ancestor of the Dalyells of Lingo in Fife, whose descendants emigrated to Australia in the 1840s.

Above the door out of the Dining Room is Magdalen Dalyell, ancestor of President Harry Truman, by William Aikman. A portrait of her husband James Menteith of Auldcathie, by the same painter, hangs on the east wall. The best painting in the house is that of Christian Shairp of Houston, granddaughter of Janet Dalyell, by Allan Ramsay.

On either side of the doors to the Morning Room are portraits by Stanley Cursiter of Eleanor Dalyell, who granted the Charter of the Binns to the National Trust for Scotland, and her husband, Colonel Gordon Loch, wearing the tabard of Unicorn Pursuivant of Arms.

Above Eleanor are portraits by Cosmo Alexander of the two younger brothers of Sir Robert Dalyell, 4th Baronet: Captain James, killed at Fort Detroit in 1763; and Captain Thomas Dalyell RN, killed in India in 1765.

The portrait of Charles II is said to be by Sir Godfrey Kneller, or possibly out of the studio of Sir Peter Lely, or by John Michael Wright.

The huge comb used by General Tam Dalyell, who vowed after the execution of Charles I never to cut his hair until the Stuarts were restored to the throne

THE HIGH HALL

In the seventeenth century, this room had three windows, smaller than the present ones, facing north and another three facing south. The rooms on this floor were all interconnected; the book passage beyond the Hall is a later addition.

The distinctive plaster ceiling is one of a series commissioned by Thomas Dalyell in 1630 for the expected visit of King Charles I in 1633. This and the ceiling in the adjoining King's Room were done by skilled Italian craftsmen, who travelled round the houses of Scotland with their moulds in the early decades of the seventeenth century. The work is attributed to Alexander White, whose name may at one time have been Alessandro Bianco. This would tally with the family tradition of commissioning Italian work.

The High Hall ceiling has a geometric design with heraldic devices, the intertwined initials of TD and IB (Thomas Dalyell, who built the house, and his wife Janet Bruce) and the Dalyell coat-of-arms. In the centre is a splendid central boss that once supported a pendant light.

Above the chimneypiece is the coat-of-arms of Charles I flanked by Prince of Wales feathers, as a compliment to the future Charles II, who was born in May 1630.

THE STAIRWAY AND BOOK PASSAGE

During the renovations at the end of the eighteenth century, this straight stone stair was inserted into a room previously known as the Stone Room.

The two landscape paintings show the house from the north and south: they are thought to be 'blueprints' for the architectural changes of the 1820s. The portrait of Magdalen Kinloch, mother-in-law of Harriet Dalyell, is of a splendid old lady clutching a tatting shuttle. She lost her sight, according to family tradition, 'in the year of Waterloo' – 1815. But this did not prevent her from continuing to indulge her passion for card-playing – to the detriment of the family fortunes.

Above left: portrait of Magdalen Kinloch. Right: Jew Dragoman at Jerusalem, by David Wilkie, 1840

The books, collected over many generations, are typical of many a laird's library. Opposite the books, note the fine etchings by the renowned Scottish artist David Wilkie (1785-1841), who was a cousin of the Dalyells.

THE KING'S ROOM

This was destined to be the bedroom of Charles I, and so it has the most elaborate of the plaster ceilings in the house. It features a running pattern of thistles and roses – a popular decoration after the Union of the Crowns in 1603 – and the four emblems of the United Kingdom: the thistle for Scotland, rose for England and Wales, harp for Ireland and fleur-de-lys for France, to which the Stuarts laid claim. Two of the nine worthies of ancient history appear twice in medallions: Alexander the Great of Macedon and David the Psalmist King. Note that the 'n' in Alexander and the 'd' of David are the wrong way round.

Above the fireplace is the royal coat-of-arms of Scotland with the English motto – another device commemorating the Union of the two kingdoms. The elaborate frieze of fruits and cherubs signifies a cornucopia of plenty – an allusion to the supposed benefits of the reign of Charles I – and in the centre of the ceiling is an elaborate boss from which to suspend a lamp.

King Charles never did see all this artistic effort. He was on his way to the Binns, travelling by sea from Burntisland to Blackness, when a sudden storm blew up and drowned 30 of his entourage. Instead of landing at Blackness, he sailed direct to Leith, the port for Edinburgh, and from there rode swiftly to London to scotch rumours that he too had drowned.

The matching wardrobes are early nineteenth-century and from an Edinburgh workshop; the open armchairs are French, Louis XV, and bear the stamp of Jean-Baptiste Meunier. In the showcase to the left of the fireplace are some beautiful Persian miniatures that Eleanor Dalyell had commissioned in Isfahan. The other showcase to the left of the bed displays a silver chatelaine's girdle, a candle snuffer and a Victorian silverwork case, all belonging to Lady Mary Dalyell.

The oil paintings are of Mary of Modena, second wife of James VII and II, and her two children, James the Old Pretender as a young boy and Princess Marie Louise, who died of smallpox at the age of 21. The small miniature is of Charles Edward Stuart, the Young Pretender, after Antonio David. The other portraits are of Gustavus Adolphus, King of Sweden, and Christian IV of Denmark, brother of Anne of Denmark, queen of James VI and I.

Below: these fine Persian miniatures were commissioned by Eleanor Dalyell in 1934

THE BINNS PARKLAND

A signposted Woodland Walk will take you through the grounds and up to the tower, from where you can enjoy the magnificent views.

The landscape was laid out between the mid-eighteenth and mid-nineteenth centuries, and was designed to produce a visual impact on visitors. Guests of the Dalyells would have entered the estate both by the present west driveway and by the east gates, which were removed in the 1960s. As their carriages drove towards the house, they would pass through contrasting landscapes – woods, then open meadows where cows grazed. New views would be revealed at every turn, culminating in the breathtaking panorama of the Firth of Forth and, finally, sight of the house itself, emerging imposingly from the surrounding trees.

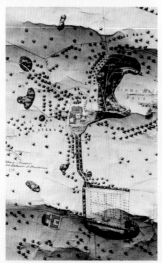

Right: an estate plan of 1857 shows the major planting of conifers and other 'Gothick' features such as gate lodges and (above) the tower, built in 1826 by Sir James Dalyell with the proceeds of a successful wager

Far right: the colour, texture and positioning of trees was an important aspect of the original design of the landscape at the Binns. Trees continue to be carefully managed by the Trust: young specimens are protected against grazing cattle by special tree crates, copies of those in the National Trust's Studley Royal estate in North Yorkshire

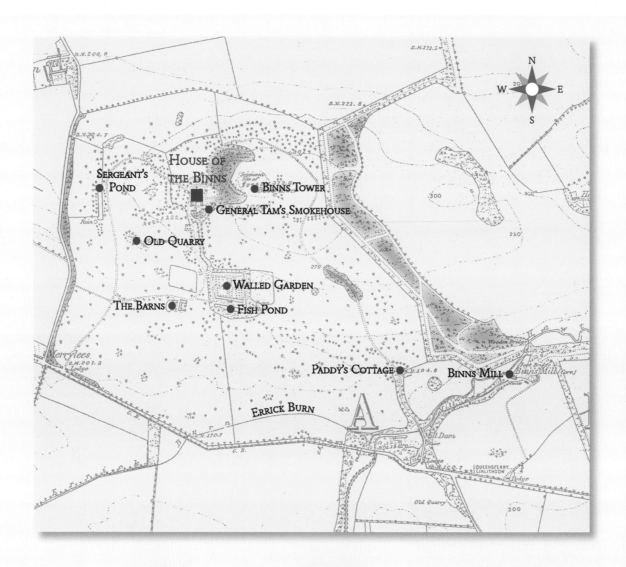

The map shows various labelled locations including:

- SERGEANT'S POND
- HOUSE OF THE BINNS
- BINNS TOWER
- GENERAL TAM'S SMOKEHOUSE
- OLD QUARRY
- WALLED GARDEN
- THE BARNS
- FISH POND
- PADDY'S COTTAGE
- BINNS MILL
- ERRICK BURN

TRACES OF THE PAST

The Ordnance Survey map of 1855 showed the Binns estate in its heyday. During the later nineteenth century many of the distinctive features of the eighteenth-century designed landscape fell into disrepair. The 1855 map is reproduced here, labelled with those features of which traces still exist.

The Peacock Tree: down the winding path from the General's Smokehouse is a huge sycamore tree, close to the garage yard. The famous peacocks and peahens that roam freely at the Binns roost here at night, sheltered from wind between the house and the hill, and out of reach of marauding foxes. Legend has it that there have always been peacocks at the Binns – they are depicted in one of the plaster ceilings in the house – and that when the peacocks go, so will the Dalyells.

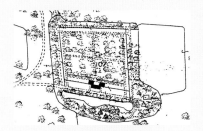

The Walled Garden: begun by Sir Robert Dalyell, 4th Baronet, and continued by his son Sir James: it was completed around 1820. Fruit and cut flowers for the house were grown here. By 1869, as shown in a report in the Binns papers, this had fallen into neglect, and the vineries that had previously existed here had disappeared. It is probable that the house had been empty or let during this period, since Sir William Dalyell served as a naval officer and later Admiral, and was rarely in residence. Recently, Tam and Kathleen Dalyell have repaired the walls, restored the potting shed and restocked the area with fruit trees.

Quarry: forming a natural amphitheatre, the site of the old quarry is still visible. Quarrying, particularly for limestone and free-stone, was carried on intensively in this area in the late sixteenth and seventeenth centuries. Nineteenth-century Ordnance Survey maps show one old quarry in West Park. Smaller quarries and rock outcrops occur on the summit of Binns Hill and north-west of the Walled Garden.

General Tam's Smokehouse: the remains of an ivy-covered grotto which was used by General Tam Dalyell, either for smoking meat and fish, or simply for relaxing with a pipe of tobacco. In the General's day there would have been extensive views from here, but this is now obscured by trees.

The Sergeant's Pond: to the west of the drive, this pond is fed by springs. It was enlarged around 1681 when the Greys were camped at the Binns and was used for watering the regiment's horses.

The Fish Pond: the canal to the south of the Walled Garden was used as a curling pond by Sir James Bruce Wilkie Dalyell. We do not know if it was ever stocked with fish. In the nineteenth century it was surrounded by an ornamental shrubbery.

Paddy's Cottage: this small chapel-like building in the Tower Park is named after Paddy Gallagher, a former soldier who hired himself out to farmers and lived here during the 1920s and 1930s.

Binns Mill: the old mill building is now just outside the boundary of NTS property. Sir Thomas Dalyell acquired the 'New Mill' in 1687 and was granted permission by a neighbouring landowner to dam the Errick Burn to feed it. A document of 1712 shows that the miller paid a yearly rent of '6 firlots of bere and 10 hens'.

The Barns: now crumbling buildings, these are thought to have been used as barracks for the Royal Scots Greys. Nineteenth-century photographs show them still in use as dwellings.

WILDLIFE

The buildings, gardens and estate at the Binns support a wide variety of wildlife throughout the year, making it a good place to check out natural sights, sounds and smells at any time of the day.

The small woods around the estate contain a wide variety of animal and plant species. Take a walk on the woodland trail by the house and before too long you will be among a rich mixture of native and non-native plant species. The rarest native plant here is the shining cranesbill, a member of the geranium family. In the summer months keep an eye out for the colourful flowering buddleia bushes, which are a favourite of many species of butterfly. Peacock butterflies can often be seen here – identify them by the large false eyes on their wings. You may also see or hear another type of peacock around this wood!

Errick Burn Wood has a wild feel to it these days, as sycamore and ash gradually replace the decaying dead elms. Alder and willow enjoy the damp conditions in the wood, as do the yellow-flowered lesser celandines and marsh marigolds. Plants associated with old woodland, such as sanicle, indicate that much of this wood is long established. Many species of birds can be found here, including visiting summer migrants such as the willow warbler and chiff chaff.

The House of the Binns is surrounded by grassland, which is grazed by cattle, sheep and rabbits – including black ones! Much of it has been improved for grazing, but pockets of wild flowers remain on slopes and thinner soils. Species such as field madder, bulbous buttercup and dovesfoot cranesbill grow here in abundance, adding colour from May onwards. You may come across small scratch holes in the turf; a sure sign of badgers foraging throughout the parkland for earthworms. Brown hares enjoy the wide open space of these grasslands, along with rabbits, a favourite prey of the buzzards that you may see soaring above you. The grasslands are also a favourite haunt of other birds, with curlew often present in large flocks, while mixed groups of goldfinch and linnet fly between the old parkland trees.

We always ask visitors to enjoy wildlife on Trust properties and to tell staff what they see so that we can continue to monitor the effects of our management on wild plants and animals.

LEGEND AND TRADITION

There are many intriguing legends and traditions surrounding the family and the Binns.

The hill above the house was, by tradition, where the Picts made their last stand against the Romans, and the figure of a Pict, a little old man in brownish garb with a hood, is said to be seen at times on the hillside gathering wood.

The pond below the hill on the west – the Sergeant's Pond – is believed to be the abode of a water sprite which seeks to lure its victims to the depths. The original pond, fed by springs and of great antiquity, was enlarged about 1681 to water the horses of the Greys.

The hillock by the gate, known as the Black Lodge, is reputed to be the abode of another spirit and it is said that horses show signs of fear when taken past it in the gloaming.

The ghost of General Tam himself, mounted on a white charger, is said to ride across the old medieval bridge over the Errick Burn and up the old drive to the house.

THE DEVIL AND TAM DALYELL

It is hardly surprising that many of the legendary tales attached to the Binns centre on the outstanding personality of General Tam Dalyell. Partisan accounts of his activities against the Covenanters have given rise to many of the hostile stories about him – particularly those telling of his 'trookings', or dealings, with the Devil.

Every night, goes one of the stories, the two played cards, the Devil usually winning. However, on one occasion the General won, and the Devil was so enraged that he hurled the card table at his opponent's head. It missed and landed in the Sergeant's Pond. It is easy to dismiss this as an amusing tale told round the fire on winter nights. But in the very dry summer of 1878 a heavy table of carved marble was revealed at the bottom of the pond, and was recovered from the mud in which it had lain for 200 years. After having been cleaned, it was discovered to be a seventeenth-century table of Carrara marble bearing a strange hoof-like mark in one corner that no cleaning will remove. The table still stands in the Laigh Hall – so you can look at it and decide for yourself whether the old story is true!

Another story tells how in the course of an argument with the General, the Devil threatened: *'I will blow down your house upon you.'* Tam replied: *'Oh no, you won't, for I will build me walls about the house to protect it.'* The Devil retorted: *'That will not avail you. I shall blow down your walls and your house forebye [as well].'* The General answered: *'You will not, for I will build me a turret at every corner to pin down the walls.'* To this day, the walls have corner turrets which serve no other purpose.

Until quite recently there used to be sung a ballad which began: *'Wha rides aroon oor hoose the nicht? Nane but Bluidy Tam.'* A long list of enquiries follows as to who had done all manner of evil deeds, with the refrain *'Nane but Bluidy Tam'* to each of them.

The General's boots of Russian leather can be seen in the Dining Room. They are said to bring water poured into them to the boil. Whenever they are taken from the house, so the legend goes, they walk, being restless to get back to the Binns. The General's son, John, took them to his home at Lingo in Fife, but every night when he took them off, they disturbed the house with their walking until they were eventually returned to the Binns, where they have remained peacefully ever since.

WHILE YOU ARE IN THE AREA ...

why not visit these nearby National Trust for Scotland properties?

Royal Burgh of Culross, Fife
Situated on the northern shore of the Forth, this picturesque royal burgh evokes Scottish life in the sixteenth and seventeenth centuries. The Palace has splendid original painted woodwork and fine furniture, and the garden contains vegetables and herbs available in the early seventeenth century. You can also visit the Town House and the Study.
Tel 0844 493 2189

Bannockburn, near Stirling
One of the most important historic sites in Scotland, this is where Robert the Bruce triumphed over the English army of Edward II in 1314. Visit the Heritage Centre to find out what inspired this great victory, and walk the battlefield under the gaze of Bruce himself, immortalised in a magnificent statue by Pilkington Jackson.
Tel 0844 493 2139

Gladstone's Land & The Georgian House, Edinburgh
Experience the contrasts of living in Old and New Town Edinburgh. Gladstone's Land is a typical seventeenth-century tenement in the Old Town, with some remarkable painted ceilings and a restored 'luckenbooth' cloth shop.

Across town, the elegant eighteenth-century Georgian House, designed by Robert Adam, reflects life for the well-to-do in the fashionable New Town, and has exquisite collections of china, silver, paintings and furniture.
Gladstone's Land: tel 0844 493 2120
Georgian House: tel 0844 493 2117

Malleny Garden, Balerno, Edinburgh
Renowned for its flamboyant plantings of old-fashioned roses and herbaceous perennials, Malleny is a beautiful and tranquil place. The garden is dominated by four magnificent clipped yew trees dating from the seventeenth century, and there is also a vegetable and herb garden as well as pleasant woodland walks.
Tel 0844 493 2123

Newhailes, Musselburgh, East Lothian
Newhailes is an amazing survival of a seventeenth-century house with eighteenth-century additions in authentic condition. The Trust has worked hard to keep the house 'untouched' by modern hands, and you can enjoy much of the original decorative scheme and furnishings. Explore, too, the fascinating eighteenth-century designed landscape.
Tel 0844 493 2125

Linlithgow Palace (Historic Scotland) and **Hopetoun House** (Hopetoun House Preservation Trust) are also very near the Binns.

FURTHER READING

Dalyell, Sir James and Beveridge, James (eds), *The Binns Papers, 1320-1864,* Edinburgh 1938.
Dalyell, Sir John Graham, *Rare and Remarkable Animals of Scotland, represented from living subjects, with practical observations on their nature,* London, 1847-8.
Dalyell, Kathleen 'Family Papers at the House of the Binns', in *Scottish Archives 2004,* Vol 10.
Peter McGowan Associates, *The Binns: Historical Landscape Survey,* Edinburgh, 1999.

ACCESS FOR ALL

The National Trust for Scotland welcomes disabled visitors. The following facilities are available at the House of the Binns:

- Designated parking spaces at house by arrangement
- Eight rooms on ground floor accessible
- 'Armchair visit' with photograph album of two rooms on upper floor
- Accessible toilet
- Information file on each room for visitors who are hard-of-hearing
- Guided tours and Braille information sheets for visually impaired visitors

THE NATIONAL TRUST FOR SCOTLAND

28 Charlotte Square, Edinburgh EH2 4ET
www.nts.org.uk   Scottish Charity No. SC 007410
The National Trust for Scotland is Scotland's leading conservation organisation. It is not a government department, but a charity supported by its membership of 300,000.

The Trust was founded in 1931 by a small group of Scots concerned at the growing threat to the country's natural and built heritage. Now, it is an influential body with more than a hundred diverse properties. Its remit, set out in various Acts of Parliament, is to promote the care and conservation of the Scottish landscape and historic buildings while providing access for the public to enjoy them.